ENCOURAGEMENT for

Students

© 2008 by Barbour Publishing, Inc.

Compiled by Kathy Shutt.

ISBN 978-1-60260-201-4

Some material previously published in *Now You're a Graduate; God Bless You, Graduate; Dream Big; Congratulations on Your Accomplishment; A Prayer for the Graduate; Good Job!; Congratulations! Now You're a Graduate; Way To Go, Grad!; For I Know the Plans I Have for You, Says the Lord; Moving Mountains; A Future of Promise; 365 Prayers for Teachers,* all published by Barbour Publishing, Inc.

Scripture quotations marked NIV are taken from the HOLY BIBLE, NEW INTERNATIONAL VERSION®. NIV®. Copyright © 1973, 1978, 1984 by International Bible Society. Used by permission of Zondervan. All rights reserved.

Scripture quotations marked NKJV are taken from the New King James Version®. Copyright © 1982 by Thomas Nelson, Inc. Used by permission. All rights reserved.

Scripture quotations marked THE MESSAGE are from ***THE MESSAGE.*** Copyright © by Eugene H. Peterson 1993, 1994, 1995, 1996, 2000, 2001, 2002. Used by permission of NavPress Publishing Group.

Published by Barbour Publishing, Inc., P.O. Box 719, Uhrichsville, Ohio 44683, www.barbourbooks.com

Our mission is to publish and distribute inspirational products offering exceptional value and biblical encouragement to the masses.

Printed in China.

ENCOURAGEMENT FOR

Students

GARBORG'S
PUBLISHING

Summer 2009

Dear Mimi-chan,
Congratulations on your graduation
from Jr. High School!

"With God all things are possible."

MATTHEW 19:26 NIV

"God is with us!" "Fear not!"
Love,
Mahiko Dua

Success consists of getting up
just more times than you fall.

OLIVER GOLDSMITH

It does not matter how slowly you go,
so long as you do not stop.

CONFUCIUS

Hitch your wagon to a star.

RALPH WALDO EMERSON

Reach high, for stars lie hidden in your soul.
Dream deep, for every dream precedes the goal.

PAMELA VAULL STARR

Life is made up of choices, not chances. It is up to you to make the right choices for your life.

CONOVER SWOFFORD

Dear Lord, hold my hand when fear threatens to overwhelm and disable me. When I feel inadequate, insignificant, or discouraged, give me the strength to keep going, the courage to stand up for what I believe in, and a desire to give You nothing less than my very best. Give me faith that conquers fear.

JENNA MILLER

Don't wait for your ship to come;
swim out to it.

ANONYMOUS

Your future is bright as the promises of God.

CONOVER SWOFFORD

Life is a series of surprises.

RALPH WALDO EMERSON

He who asks a question is a fool for five minutes;
he who does not ask a question remains a fool forever.

CHINESE PROVERB

Choose always the way that seems best,
however rough it may be.

Pythagoras

"But" is a fence over which few leap.

GERMAN PROVERB

All dreams can come true—
if we have the courage to pursue them.

WALT DISNEY

We must make the choices that enable us to fulfill the deepest capacities of ourselves.

THOMAS MERTON

Be strong in the grace that
is in Christ Jesus.

2 TIMOTHY 2:1 NIV

Take time to determine the way you will live your life.
But once you know the way you should go,
let nothing distract you from your path.

ELLYN SANNA

Most people never run far enough on their first wind to find out if they've got a second. Give your dreams all you've got, and you'll be amazed at the energy that comes out of you.

WILLIAM JAMES

Sometimes it's not for us to know
God's "why" for certain things.

CONOVER SWOFFORD

Aim high. Shoot for the stars.
Don't settle for anything
less than your best.

ELLYN SANNA

Just waiting for the Lord to do work is often hard to do. But we must wait for His good time. He knows what's best for you.

CONOVER SWOFFORD

Dear Lord, I know that life is not always going to be a bed of roses and that sometimes I will experience pain, sadness, loneliness, and fear. Help me not to dwell on these things and allow them to destroy me, but to trust in You for peace and happiness. Give me the ability to be thankful for the little things in life and for joy that withstands any storm.

JENNA MILLER

Plan your future carefully.
That's where you're going to spend
the rest of your life.

ANONYMOUS

The future lies before us to do with as we will. The possibilities are limitless; the responsibility is overwhelming; and the anticipation is absolutely breathtaking.

CONOVER SWOFFORD

Why not go out on a limb?
Isn't that where the fruit is?

FRANK SCULLY

All life is an experiment. The more experiments you make, the better.

RALPH WALDO EMERSON

Why should we be in such desperate haste to succeed, and in such desperate enterprises? If a man does not keep pace with his companions, perhaps it is because he hears a different drummer.

HENRY DAVID THOREAU

Learn while you're young, and not while you're
old, that a good education is better than gold;
for silver and gold will all melt away,
but a good education will never decay.

ANONYMOUS

Never part with your illusions. Without dreams you may continue to exist, but you have ceased to live.

MARK TWAIN

God does not demand the impossible,
but He tells us to do what we can and to ask for
what we cannot do; then He helps us to be able.

COUNCIL OF TRENT

You will rejoice, and no one
will take away your joy.

JOHN 16:22 NIV

The will to win, the desire to succeed,
the urge to reach your full potential. . .these are
the keys that will unlock the door to personal excellence.

EDDIE ROBINSON

I don't know what your destiny will be, but one thing I know: The only ones among you who will be really happy are those who sought and found how to serve.

DR. ALBERT SCHWEITZER

Look at life through the windshield,
not the rearview mirror.

BYRD BAGGETT

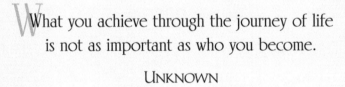

What you achieve through the journey of life
is not as important as who you become.

UNKNOWN

The future belongs to those who
believe in the beauty of their dreams.

ELEANOR ROOSEVELT

Dear Lord, in my quest for success and accomplishment, help me to remember that to truly be successful, I need to develop the ability to learn from my mistakes, be a servant to others, and put my best efforts into whatever I do.

JENNA MILLER

Be decisive. Don't be afraid to do wrong.
We all make mistakes, but you'll never accomplish
anything if you never act at all.

ELLYN SANNA

The important thing is
not to stop questioning.

ALBERT EINSTEIN

Success is measured not so much by the position that one has reached in life as by the obstacles which he has overcome trying to succeed.

BOOKER T. WASHINGTON

Do a little more each day than
you think you possibly can.

LOWELL THOMAS

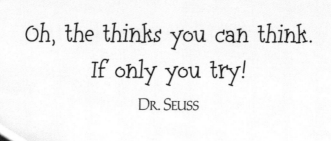

Oh, the thinks you can think.
If only you try!

DR. SEUSS

This above all: To thine own self be true:
And it must follow, as the night the day,
Thou canst not then be false to any man.

WILLIAM SHAKESPEARE

Everyone has talent. What is rare
is the courage to follow that
talent. . .where it leads.

ERICA JONG

This shall be my parting word:
Know what you want to do—then do it!

ERNEST SCHUMANN-HEINK

So do not throw away your confidence;
it will be richly rewarded. You need to persevere
so that when you have done the will of God,
you will receive what he has promised.

HEBREWS 10:35-36 NIV

Hide not your talents.
They for use were made.
What's a sundial in the shade?

BENJAMIN FRANKLIN

The best path to follow through life
is to step in the footsteps of Jesus.

CONOVER SWOFFORD

If Columbus had turned back, no one would have blamed him. Of course, no one would have remembered him either.

UNKNOWN

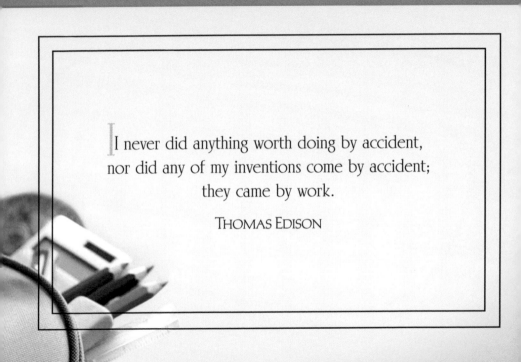

I never did anything worth doing by accident,
nor did any of my inventions come by accident;
they came by work.

THOMAS EDISON

Keep away from people who try to belittle your ambitions. Small people always do that, but the really great make you feel that you, too, can become great.

MARK TWAIN

Dear Lord, my future at this point in my life is very uncertain. I don't know where I'll be in a year or in ten years. Continue to remind me that You hold my future in Your hands and that You have a plan for my life that exceeds all of my feeble expectations.

JENNA MILLER

Pray to God, but keep rowing to shore.

RUSSIAN PROVERB

The noblest question in the world is, "What good may I do in it?"

BENJAMIN FRANKLIN

Doubt sees the obstacles; faith sees the way.
Doubt sees the darkest night; faith sees the day.
Doubt dreads to take a step;
faith soars on high. Doubt questions,
"Who believes?"; faith answers, "I."

ANONYMOUS

The secret to success is to do
the common things uncommonly well.

JOHN D. ROCKEFELLER JR.

Life is like a baseball game.
You do not have to succeed seven out of ten times,
and you can still make the all-star team.

ANONYMOUS

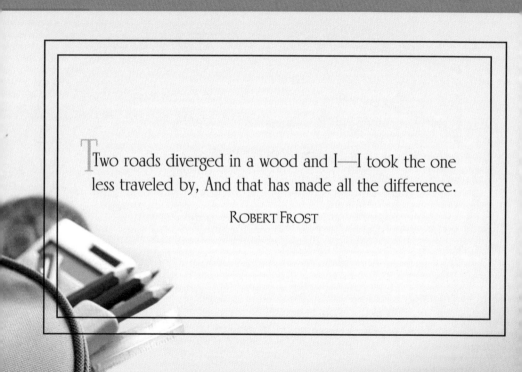

Two roads diverged in a wood and I—I took the one less traveled by, And that has made all the difference.

ROBERT FROST

Vision is the art of
seeing things invisible.

JONATHAN SWIFT

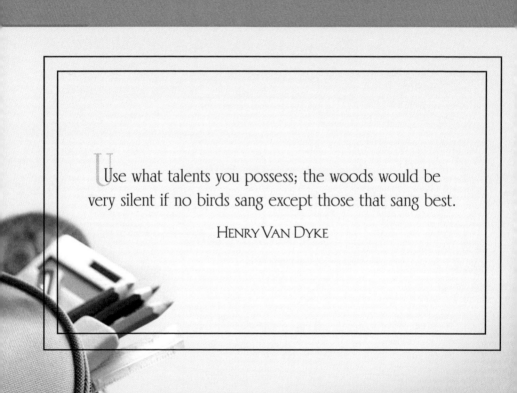

Use what talents you possess; the woods would be
very silent if no birds sang except those that sang best.

HENRY VAN DYKE

Let us fix our eyes on Jesus,
the author and perfecter of our faith.

HEBREWS 12:2 NIV

The great thing in this world is not so much where we are but in what direction we are going.

ANONYMOUS

It is a mistaken idea that greatness
and great success mean the same thing.

ANONYMOUS

What I must do is all that concerns me,
not what the people think.

RALPH WALDO EMERSON

Every person you meet knows something you don't.
Learn from them.

H. JACKSON BROWN

To have what you want is riches;
but to be able to do without is power.

GEORGE MCDONALD

God, I can only pray that I'm living a life that is pleasing to You. You have given me everything and continue to be with me each step of the way, through my every journey.

LARISSA NYGREN

"Begin at the beginning,"
the king said, gravely, "and go on
till you come to the end; then stop."

LEWIS CARROLL, from *Alice in Wonderland*

The future belongs to the dreamers, but only the dreamers who believe so much in their dreams that they are willing to wake up and achieve them.

CONOVER SWOFFORD

Never let anyone tell you that it can't be done.
Maybe what cannot be done by anyone else is
the reason God created you to do it.

CONOVER SWOFFORD

Choose a job you love, and you will never have to work a day in your life.

CONFUCIUS

Make your work to be in
keeping with your purpose.

LEONARDO DA VINCI

Don't let someone's criticism alter your opinion of yourself. Whatever they are criticizing is sure to be the best of what makes you an individual.

CONOVER SWOFFORD

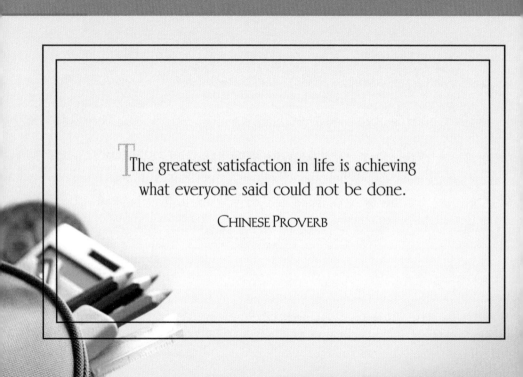

The greatest satisfaction in life is achieving
what everyone said could not be done.

CHINESE PROVERB

Never mistake motion for action.

ERNEST HEMINGWAY

The Spirit of truth. . .
will guide you into all truth.

JOHN 16:13 NIV

W Wisdom is knowing what to do next.
Skill is knowing how to do it. Virtue is doing it.

THOMAS JEFFERSON

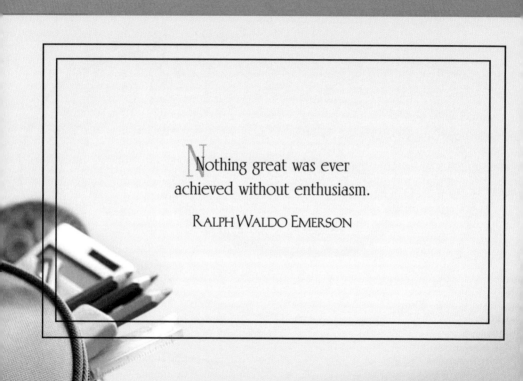

Nothing great was ever
achieved without enthusiasm.

RALPH WALDO EMERSON

A piece of the miracle process has been reserved for each of us.

JIM ROHN

The beginning is the most important
part of the week.

PLATO

Success is the journey,
not the destination.

ANONYMOUS

God, may my life be in some way a reflection
of You, Lord, that others may see in me
Your light and heart. Amen.

LARISSA NYGREN

Every time you make a choice you are turning
the central part of you, the part that chooses,
into something a little different than what it was before.

C. S. Lewis

Do what you love.

HENRY DAVID THOREAU

Nobody gets to live life backwards.
Look ahead—that's where your future lies.

ANN LANDERS

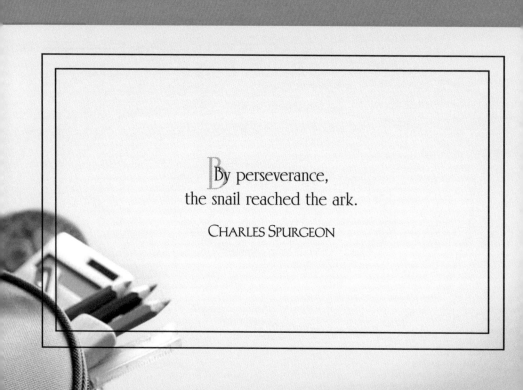

By perseverance,
the snail reached the ark.

CHARLES SPURGEON

If you can't excel with talent,
triumph with effort.

DAVE WEINBAUM

I find the great thing in this world is not so much where we stand as in what direction we are moving.

OLIVER WENDELL HOLMES

The reason some [people] do not succeed is because their wishbone is where their backbone ought to be.

ANONYMOUS

Don't put off for tomorrow what you can do today, because if you enjoy it today, you can do it again tomorrow.

JAMES A. MICHENER

The LORD will guide you always; he will satisfy your needs. . . . You will be like a well-watered garden, like a spring whose waters never fail.

ISAIAH 58:11 NIV

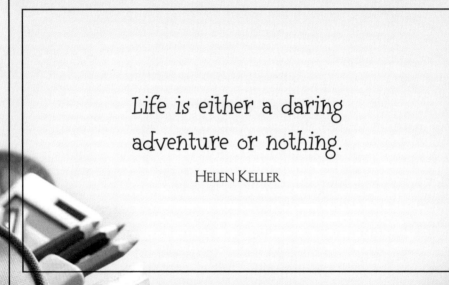

Life is either a daring
adventure or nothing.

HELEN KELLER

Let him who would move the
world first move himself.

SENECA

The world cares very little about what a man or woman knows; it is what the man or woman is able to do that counts.

BOOKER T. WASHINGTON

Every man's life is a fairy tale,
written by God's fingers.

HANS CHRISTIAN ANDERSON

Early to bed and early to rise makes
a man healthy, wealthy, and wise.

BENJAMIN FRANKLIN

Praise be to our wonderful Lord
for His bountiful blessings!

LARISSA NYGREN

Fortune favors the bold
but abandons the timid.

LATIN PROVERB

Everything that is done in this
world is done by hope.

MARTIN LUTHER

To one who has faith, no explanation is necessary.
To one without faith, no explanation is possible.

ST. THOMAS AQUINAS

Perseverance is what turns failure into success.
It isn't failure—it's just a way that didn't work.

CONOVER SWOFFORD

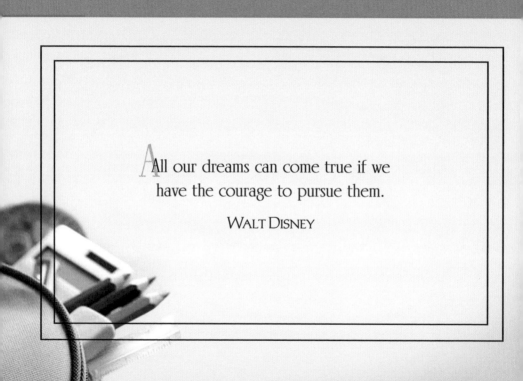

All our dreams can come true if we
have the courage to pursue them.

WALT DISNEY

If you stop every time a dog barks,
your road will never end.

ARABIAN PROVERB

Profound joy of the heart is like a magnet that indicates the path of life. One has to follow it, even though one enters into a way full of difficulties.

MOTHER TERESA

What we might think of as speed bumps in our life's roads are usually only God's way of slowing us down enough to get our attention.

CONOVER SWOFFORD

Trust in the LORD with all your heart and lean not on your own understanding; in all your ways acknowledge him, and he will make your paths straight.

PROVERBS 3:5-6 NIV

As you look to the future, don't be afraid to dream.
God will use your dreams if you give them to Him.
Dare to dream big dreams and then wait on God.
You may be surprised what He will do.

ELLYN SANNA

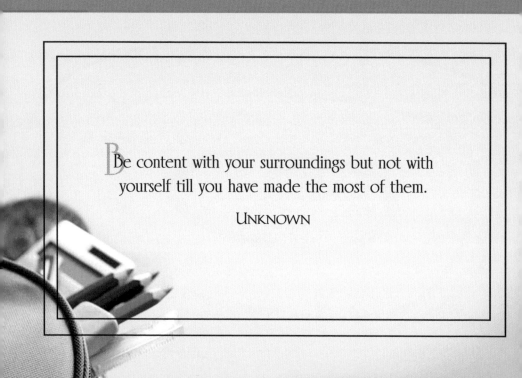

Be content with your surroundings but not with yourself till you have made the most of them.

UNKNOWN

Life affords no greater pleasure
than overcoming obstacles.

Unknown

May you have the courage to let
yourself drop into the hands of God.

ELLYN SANNA

Four steps to achievement: 1. Plan purposefully.
2. Prepare prayerfully. 3. Proceed positively.
4. Pursue persistently.

WILLIAM A. WARD

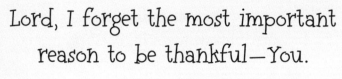

Lord, I forget the most important reason to be thankful—You.

LARISSA NYGREN

If the only prayer you said in your whole life
was "Thank You," that would suffice.

MEISTER ECKHART

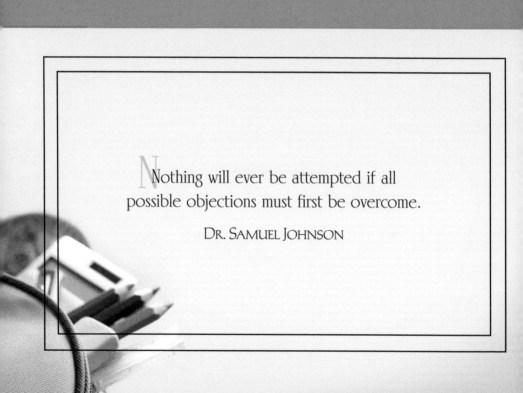

Nothing will ever be attempted if all
possible objections must first be overcome.

DR. SAMUEL JOHNSON

Learning is a treasure that will
follow its owner everywhere.

CHINESE PROVERB

When love and skill work together,
expect a masterpiece.

JOHN RUSKIN

Every great achievement was
once considered impossible.

UNKNOWN

Life is a balancing act.

CONOVER SWOFFORD

The secret of success is
the constancy of purpose.

BENJAMIN DISRAELI

Count your blessings instead of your crosses, Count your gains instead of your losses. Count your joys instead of your woes, Count your friends instead of your foes. Count your health instead of your wealth.

IRISH BLESSING

Seek the LORD your God,
you will find him if you look for him with all
your heart and with all your soul.

DEUTERONOMY 4:29 NIV

Education is the most powerful weapon
you can use to change the world.

NELSON ROLIHLAHLA MANDELA

We know what we are,
but know not what we may be.

WILLIAM SHAKESPEARE

The secret of happiness is not in doing what one likes but in liking what one has to do.

SIR JAMES MATTHEW BARRIE

The world of tomorrow belongs to
the person who has the vision today.

ROBERT SCHULLER

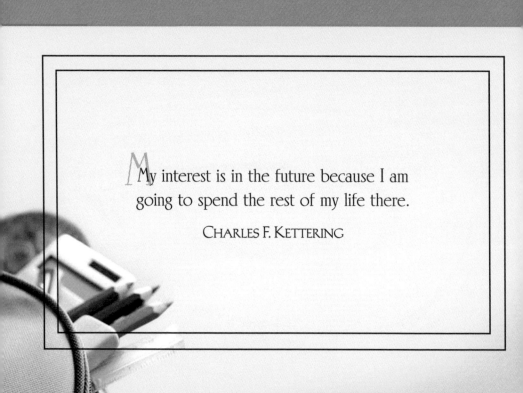

My interest is in the future because I am going to spend the rest of my life there.

CHARLES F. KETTERING

Lord God, build in me a heart of cheerfulness that will get me through the tough school days that seem interminable. Amen.

UNKNOWN

The only place where success comes before work is in the dictionary.

VIDAL SASSOON

Do not think about who you have been.
Who are you now? Who have you decided to become?

ANTHONY ROBBINS

Don't aim for success if you want it; just do what you love and believe in, and it will come naturally.

DAVID FROST

A successful person is a dreamer
whom someone believed in.

UNKNOWN

Successful people are not gifted;
they just work hard and then succeed on purpose.

G. K. NIELSON

The difference between a successful person and others is not a lack of strength, not a lack of knowledge, but rather a lack of will.

UNKNOWN

We must never be afraid to get
too far, for success lies just beyond.

MARCEL PROUST

The elevator to success is out of order.
You'll have to use the stairs. . .one at a time.

JOE GIRARD

Be content with who you are, and don't put on airs. God's strong hand is on you; he'll promote you at the right time. Live carefree before God; he is most careful with you.

1 PETER 5:6-7 MSG

Change is the law of life.
And those who look only to the past or present
are certain to miss the future.

JOHN F. KENNEDY

Courage is being afraid
but going on anyhow.

DAN RATHER

Good character. . .it is not given to us.
We have to build it piece by piece—by thought,
choice, courage, and determination.

H. JACKSON BROWN

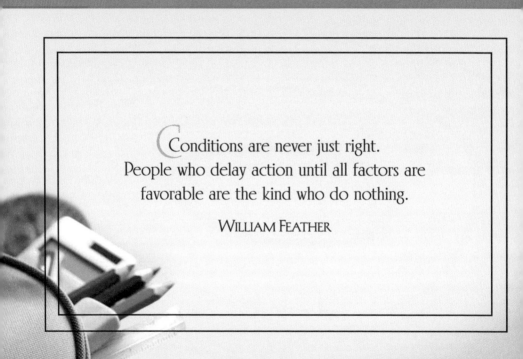

Conditions are never just right.
People who delay action until all factors are
favorable are the kind who do nothing.

WILLIAM FEATHER

The roots of true achievement lie in the will to become the best you can be.

HAROLD TAYLOR

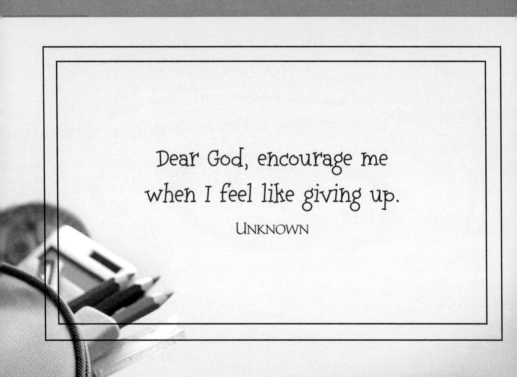

Dear God, encourage me
when I feel like giving up.

UNKNOWN

Happy are those who dream dreams and are willing to pay the price to make them come true.

ANONYMOUS

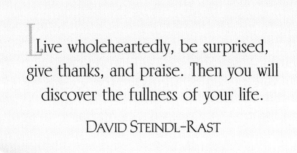

Live wholeheartedly, be surprised,
give thanks, and praise. Then you will
discover the fullness of your life.

DAVID STEINDL-RAST

We find in life exactly
what we put into it.

RALPH WALDO EMERSON

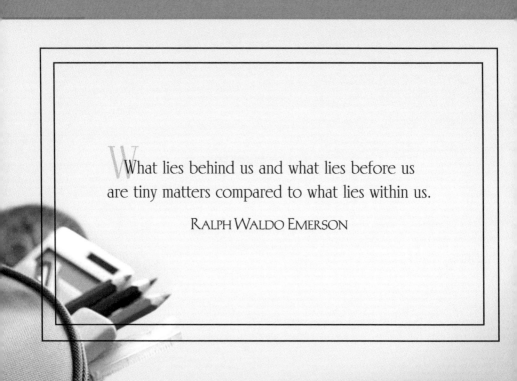

What lies behind us and what lies before us
are tiny matters compared to what lies within us.

RALPH WALDO EMERSON

Luck is a matter of
preparation meeting opportunity.

Oprah Winfrey

Do what you can, with what
you have, where you are.

THEODORE ROOSEVELT

Do not wait for extraordinary situations
to do good; try to use ordinary situations.

JEAN PAUL RICHTER

A wise man will make more
opportunities than he finds.

FRANCIS BACON

Seek first the kingdom of God and His righteousness,
and all these things shall be added to you.

MATTHEW 6:33 NKJV

The value of life lies not in the length of days,
but in the use we make of them.

MICHEL DE MONTAIGNE

Be not afraid of growing slowly;
be afraid only of standing still.

CHINESE PROVERB

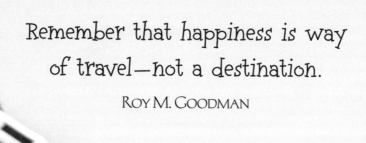

Remember that happiness is way
of travel—not a destination.

Roy M. Goodman

I cannot give you the formula for success,
but I can give you the formula for failure, which is:
Try to please everybody.

HERBERT B. SWOPE

God will never, never, never let us down if
we have faith and put our trust in Him.
He will always look after us.

MOTHER TERESA

Heavenly Father, Thank You for laughter and joy in my school day. Thank You for a sense of humor and fun times. Amen.

UNKNOWN

A champion is someone who
gets up even when he can't.

UNKNOWN

To be what we are, and to become what we
are capable of becoming, is the only end of life.

ROBERT LOUIS STEVENSON

Character cannot be developed in
ease and quiet. Only through experience of trial
and suffering can the soul be strengthened,
ambition inspired, and success achieved.

HELEN KELLER

The first step toward change is awareness.
The second step is acceptance.

NATHANIEL BRANDEN

Life is an ongoing process.
Every day is an opportunity
to learn something new.

CONOVER SWOFFORD

God gave us two ends—one to sit on and one to think with. Success depends on which one you use; heads, you win—tails, you lose.

ANONYMOUS

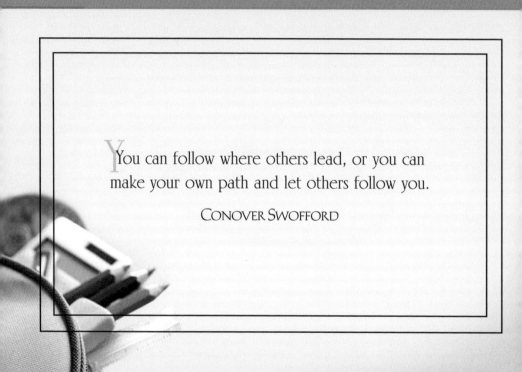

You can follow where others lead, or you can make your own path and let others follow you.

CONOVER SWOFFORD

We must live in the present
in such a way that we are not
afraid to face our future.

CONOVER SWOFFORD

The LORD your God will make you
abound in all the work of your hand.

DEUTERONOMY 30:9 NKJV

There are only two ways to live your life.
One is as though nothing is a miracle.
The other is as though everything is a miracle.

ALBERT EINSTEIN

Always be a first-rate version
of yourself, instead of a second-rate
version of somebody else.

JUDY GARLAND

I just want to do God's will. And He's allowed me to go up the mountain. And I've looked over, and I've seen the Promised Land.

MARTIN LUTHER KING JR.

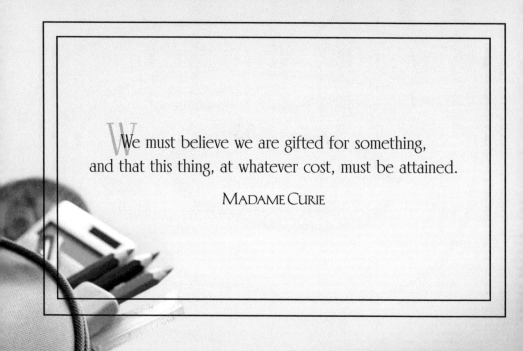

We must believe we are gifted for something,
and that this thing, at whatever cost, must be attained.

MADAME CURIE

Be nice to people on your way
up because you'll meet them
on your way down.

<small>WILSON MIZNER</small>

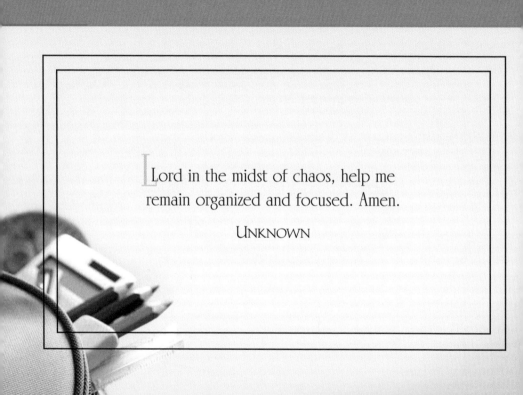

Lord in the midst of chaos, help me remain organized and focused. Amen.

UNKNOWN

I cannot change the whole world,
but I can change a small part of it.

KAY FLORENTINO

Worry is interest paid on trouble before it falls due.

W. R. INGE

They can conquer
who believe they can.

RALPH WALDO EMERSON

The future belongs to those who
believe in the beauty of their dreams.

ELEANOR ROOSEVELT

Character is what you
are in the dark.

DWIGHT MOODY

Self-confidence is the first
requisite to great undertakings.

DR. SAMUEL JOHNSON

You cannot discover new oceans unless you have
the courage to lose sight of the shore.

UNKNOWN

Vision without action is a daydream.
Action without vision is a nightmare.

JAPANESE PROVERB

I will instruct you and teach you in the way you should go; I will guide you with My eye.

PSALM 32:8 NKJV

The only real failure is to quit.

ANONYMOUS

Nothing lasts forever—not the good times
and, thank God, not the bad times.

CONOVER SWOFFORD

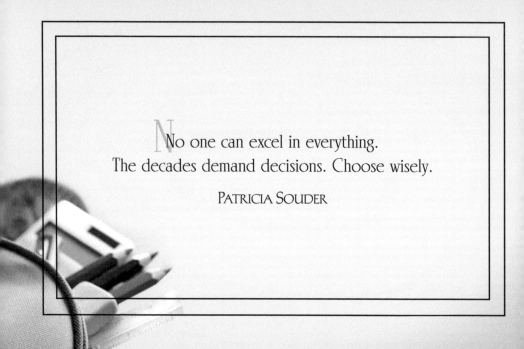

No one can excel in everything.
The decades demand decisions. Choose wisely.

PATRICIA SOUDER

Change is difficult but
often essential to survival.

LES BROWN

Yes, you can be a dreamer and a doer, too,
if you will remove one word from
your vocabulary: Impossible.

ROBERT SCHULLER

God give us the grace to accept with serenity the things that cannot be changed, courage to change the things which should be changed, and the wisdom to distinguish the one from the other.

REINHOLD NIEBUHR